It's Been A Journey

Talibah Chikwendu

BookLeaf
Publishing

India | USA | UK

Presentation by *BookLeaf Publishing*

Web: www.bookleafpub.com

E-mail: info@bookleafpub.com

ISBN: 9789363317673

First edition 2024

ACKNOWLEDGEMENT

Thanks to all the poets, teachers and friends who inspired and supported my work by example and through feedback. You have helped me find the confidence to expand my voice and share my hidden spaces.

PREFACE

I have published two small collections of poems in the past. I liked those poems, but felt many of the works lacked depth and feeling. This collection represents a move into a new phase—embracing the truth: Poetry is the medium that allows me to convey what is in my soul.

My essays and commentary are where I share my thoughts and understanding of the world. My fiction is where I put my dreams and fears. I finally realize poetry is where I feel—fully, honestly, and completely. It is in this collection that I put those vulnerable places and feelings on display.

These poems are a quick sketch of my journey of love, pain, epiphany, growth, healing and awakening in my "adult" life drawn from my active memory. Not every point was touched… there are more poems and more subjects that can be and have been written. These are the ones that emerged as this book was conceived and organized.

The goal of the selected poems is to connect
with and inspire the reader to embrace all their
lives bring them, because it is by going through
experiences and feelings that we get to healing
and growth.

*"Even when reflected in imperfect words, the
truth holds its own power."*

-Unknown

CONTENTS

The First Kiss of my 17th Year

I don't remember the situation exactly…

Was it the day you dropped me off
at the top of Kinross
To keep our wild ride
Through busy Colombo streets a secret?

Or when I met you outside the stadium
After the first rugby match I'd ever see,
you still damp
from post-game excitement?

Or if it was in the back row
during Audrey Rose?
There was kissing there,
but I am certain those were not our first.

Or when a group of us,
thumbing our noses at curfew
on a beautiful beach under the night sky…
Wait, was that you I kissed that night?

Your kiss, this kiss, was not my first kiss,
but it was the first one after my 17th birthday.
And while I know it was not my first,
It is the one I vividly remember.

I'd kissed Peter the summer before
At the end of our camp session.
But it's a blip in my memory only because
It took place in front of my dad,
Whose head I thought was going to explode.
But I don't remember the kiss.

I'm pretty sure I kissed
Ty and Craig and Avery and Snoop,
and Ross and definitely kissed Bobby a lot.
But I don't remember those kisses,
Just that they happened.
But that kiss with you, I still feel it.

Your lips were soft but a little dry
so they tickled a bit.
Your mouth touched mine, slowly and gently;
I closed my eyes, too young to realize I should
watch.
Your mouth opened on mine and I almost
giggled
As you grazed my lower lip with your teeth.

I thought: no one has done that before.
Your tongue touched mine, tip to tip; I giggled
then.
We got better at it before summer's end.
By the time I was to take my leave
I was head over heels for you and

plotting how to be left behind.

I realized
I had to return home.
I have missed you since then and
cherish every text, call and visit we share.
What we have is special, even if this is it.
And I still have the kiss.

Ode to My Ex-Husband

Happily, he's gone.

We Didn't Last

The first time we made love
It was to a song already special to me.
What was between us that afternoon,
Had a life of its own.
Every touch, sensation, emotion,
I can still call to life at will.

You knew it too.
It's why I was always aware
You were arriving at my door.
The gentle melody of the song reached my ears
first,
Drawing me outside to greet you,
simultaneously
Pulling me into that remembered frenzy.

It's been years since
I've seen you, talked to you.
I can't recall, with clarity,
An image of your face.

But still, from the opening bars of "6-String
Poet,"
I can feel your lips on my breasts,
The sweat between our bodies,
Hear my name on your labored breath,

And become swept away in that passion.

We didn't last,
But this memory did.

Healing

He raped me.
That is what you call it
When someone imposes their will
On your person
And you have dissented the
intrusion,
Have not shared the desire,
Or the interest.
When you said "No" and "Don't."
When your choice in the matter
Was taken away, treated as irrelevant.
Yeah, rape is what you call it.

It took me years to accept
That a man I'd known longer than
My bestie,
From whom I'd learned much,
And with whom I'd built much,
Regarded me as a thing he was
Entitled to possess.
That he felt my body was his to take,
That our work and play
(and what I thought was friendship)
Meant he'd earned access to penetration.

Until I named it,
And accepted the forced entrance,
The pain of it lived in me as shame.
Carrying it by myself it grew massive,
Overwhelming, blotting out my light.
I hid from others and myself,
Shutting out peace, joy and love;
Seeking contentment in
silence and solitude.
Failing, my soul lay dormant,
waiting to die.

You cannot heal
A wound you don't acknowledge.
You can't recognize
An injury you do not name.
Each day a piece of that dormant me
Flickered out, dried to dust and drifted away.
Then one day, and I don't know where I found
the strength or courage,
I named it:
Rape.

Admitting it to myself was hard,
And it didn't lift the shame.
But it shone a light on my dark places,
Illuminating the harm,
Showing me what was missing,
Building a longing for better, more.

To get there, I had to tear down the shame,
Which only happens when you tell another.
I had to say the words out loud:
"A man I trusted as an old friend,
raped me in my home."

I was afraid the first time I said it,
But my shame was not reflected.
Instead the harm was illumined,
And healing began.
It was a while before I said it again,
But this time I was stronger.
Good thing, because while shame wasn't
reflected,
Condemnation and anger were.
Even that made me stronger,
Helping me forgive myself for
Hiding in shame for so long.
Helping my light to brighten.

I have shared it lately,
In more places and spaces.
And share it here,
to fully break the remnants
of the bowl of shame my soul rested in.
My light is no longer a pile of dying embers,
But is too bright to be contained
And flows freely out of and around me.
I again feel deserving of

And ready to
Embrace the joy and love to be found.
Let living resume.

Time Cropped

My best friend is dying.
Not like we all are,
a little every day,
subtracting one heartbeat at a time
from our stockpile of thumps.
Not rapidly, but imminently …
Dropping bowls full of heartbeats
with each breath he takes.
Time cropped,
his new limits so close
I can't stop seeing him bumping them.

For three decades plus
he has backed my plays.
Let his heart break amidst my sobs
each time my world fell apart, and
found ways to put the smile
back on my face.
Reminding me I am enough…
and don't have to be strong or
go it alone.

For over three decades
he has loved me unconditionally
more than even my parents or child.
He has held my secrets and

trusted me with his.
The world, especially my world,
is better because he is in it.

My best friend is dying.
He knows because he told me.
He continues interventions
but has not embraced hope they can help.
So he doesn't talk about it.
We don't talk about it.
We keep circling the elephant,
staying connected yet distant.

So I have no one…
No one to cry with.
No one whose heart will break
amidst sobs as my world crumbles.
What will the world, my world,
be without him?

But how selfish is that?
How can I think of what I need?
Probably because he won't let me help.
He won't let me sit by his bed,
bring him sustenance, wipe his tears.
Let my heart break amidst his sobs.
He doesn't want anyone to watch
him slip away.

He doesn't want to see or leave us broken with
that memory.
But to witness is to share the pain,
the grief, the wonder of it all.

My best friend is dying.
I want his last days to be his choices,
to give control where there is so little.
I don't want him to go at all
but definitely not before he is gone,
and absolutely not unattended.
My small world is shrinking.
And I foresee going forward alone.
I know I must, and will, but
How much heart is required to sustain life?

Hero's Journey

We sail away
Because we must…
Must venture
From familiarity
From shelter
Out into depths
Of the unknown.

We cast about…
The further out we float
Leads to struggle,
Sinking
Until we relax
Into treading,
Then grow
Into swimming and
Returning to the vessel,
New.

Do we ever go back
To the port where
We started?
Or go forward
To new adventures,
Different challenges,
Explosive growth?

We must go forward
Because in knowledge
We can navigate
Through the spaces
We inhabit.
And dream.
For it isn't safety
We seek,
But the uncertainty and
Joy of
Freedom.

When Will We Ever Be Brave?

Soaring and swirling
With crashes, smooth melodies and
Sounds so soft they're almost silent,
Our anthem is
Musically glorious.
Done well
It uplifts my spirit
In ways only music can.

But I am saddened
At its end
Because the closing lyrics
Trouble–no dismay–me.
Will we ever be
"The land of the free" or
"The home of the brave?"

Will our shores ever be rid
Of the stench of slavery?
From human trafficking to
Incarcerated workers
People still profit from the
Sale of human flesh and the
Un- or under- compensated
Sweat of their brows.

Will our bravery ever encompass
Doing what is right
Over what's popular or
Expedient?
Will we ever choose to
Do without so others can have some
Of what all humans need?
Will we ever see the dignity
Simple sustenance–
A place to live, regular meals,
Basic amenities–
Contribute, and care enough
To be BRAVE enough to provide it?

The anthem was well chosen.
Designed to represent a country
At the forefront of what is
Right and good–for and about–humanity.
But it has failed and
Continues to fail
To live up to its promises
To and about us.

Until the braver angels
Buzzing about our shoulders
Shout forcefully
In our collective ears
That we must give our best
For our fellow humans,

Instead of proud,
This amazing song
Will leave me sad.

I Can Barely Hold The Tears

(Ode to Stop and Frisk)

I can't unsee it.
Like the movement of a spider
Floating down the wall in my peripheral
Every time I see your face
It's there.
I can't shake it
I can barely hold the tears.

Superimposed over the smile you give me
Or the twinkle in your eye,
it's like an apparition:
The hands on you,
The look of unearned fear in the face of torture,
The violation and helplessness.
I can barely hold the tears.

But you are here, smiling at me.
Head tilted gently in the question:
"Why are you so sad?"
I can barely hold the tears.

It wasn't right. It isn't right.
It can't ever be right.
Because you are here, I see this.

I can't console you or remove this fist of hurt
from my heart.
I can fight for change,
But I am powerless to stop it or make it right.
I can barely hold the tears.

Though it won't help…
Maybe I shouldn't try.

Finding Hope

A man once told me
"Hope hurts too much!"
I hadn't considered
the possibility.
My every breath
is drawn
in the face of hope.

The refusal of hope
Can't be unheard.
My heart breaks
considering it.
Hope is
What puts one of my feet
in front of the other.

What seemed
inconceivable
I immediately understood.
Hope and attachment
repeatedly replaced with
disappointment
equals despair.

In understanding
I was overcome

with wonder and despair…
Who can live in
a world without hope?
Isn't that infinitely
More painful?

Captured Haiku

It took me too long to realize…

I could not save you.
I cannot save anyone.
It is not my lane.

So why does it hurt so much to fail?

World Changers

I see you Kings.
Locked down.
Prisoners in a war
That captured you
Before you knew
Who and what you were fighting.

Struggle finally abated,
You wait.
Your minds now free.
Soaring to the places
You are creating in your dreams
Until you can
Raise and live them outside.

Visions this clear are infectious.
Spreading faster than the common cold
And leaving the ill unwilling to be cured …
Fighting instead to infect as many others as they
can.
Beautiful dreams manifested enrich us all.

Sit peacefully Kings.
Power will soon flow
Freely through the floodgates you've opened.
You were never alone in this.

Long before now, we went with you,
On this leg, we go with you again.
Valuing and cherishing
Each step you take
To soar above it all
Into the lands
Formed by your dreams and
Nurtured by your souls.

Heart Exposed

Motherhood
Off the table
At nineteen.

It was a relief
Really
Coming with an answer
For seven years
Of suffering.

So surprised
Couldn't fully describe
Finding life growing
Where docs said it couldn't.
Neither could anxiety.

There wasn't preparation—
Given or possible—
For the sheer panic and
Overwhelming love
Grasped upon seeing
My heart—6 pounds, 18 inches
Of smiling sunshine–
Outside my body.

Terrified
Is how I lived.
Feeling inadequate,
Deficient, incapable …
Could this delicate example
Of divine brilliance
Survive in my care?

Unsure but determined and
Fueled by love,
I learned how to live
In perpetual fear.
Unable to protect
My heart.
Unable to save my own life
As my heart roams the world.

Originally too small to move or
Protect itself;
It's now capable of
Navigating independently and being
Too far away to watch.
Still overwhelmed with love,
Pride and delight,
I no longer live terrified,
Just exposed.

My Little One

He gives without knowing
That it's special.
Without an awareness
Of how much that means.

To him it is just something he can do
So he does it.
He doesn't know
How special he is.

He is wrapped in a light of red and gold
With purple streaks of energy
That whizz off him.
It is amazing to watch.

He is always moving
Ticking things off a To-Do List
Only he can see.
I smile seeing him in action.

He is my little one.
Who knows his worth
But not yet his value.
Without a right to, I look at him with pride.

One day he will be unveiled
So the world can witness
All his growth and goodness
And embrace how special he is.

There's Room For More

I miss you.
Every day I miss you.
Every day I think of something,
encounter something,
feel something
I want to share with you.

And I can't.
Which makes me sad and lonely.
Which makes me feel ungrateful
Because I had time with you
Made memories with you
Loved and was loved by you.

I was blessed.
Nothing can take that away.
But I still miss you
In the everyday.

I miss you when
there are tears to cry
But your chest is not
there to receive them
And your arms are not
there to bring comfort.

I miss you when the day is long
But I cannot hear
your deep, gentle voice
Telling me anything,
Soothing me with sound and touch.

I miss you
Because I can't
see you with my eyes,
Because I can't
weave my fingers with yours
Because I can't
caress your lips with mine
Because I can't
press my body to yours.

Every day I miss you.
But the hole you left,
almost 20 years ago
Has finally gotten small enough
To make room for more.

I will always miss you.
But maybe
I will find a new blessing.
It will never be you.
But I don't want it to be.

They Stand Alone

What I really miss are hugs.
Maybe kisses …
But yes, definitely hugs.

That feeling of being engulfed
in the essence of another:
their scent, rhythms of heart and breath,
their warmth.

That sense of being
safe and at home
in the moment of embrace.

The ability to mutually support
your weakness with their strength.

That sharing of intimacies
between us …
those of living, hope, dreams, togetherness…

I miss the peacefulness of hugs.
They are complete–a whole thing.

They are everything…
not the start of something else.
A hug is all it is

and everything there is at the same time.

What I really miss is hugs
Maybe kisses…
But yes, definitely hugs.

Wary

I try to remember
"A thing is what it is and nothing else."
But sometimes that's hard
With a compliment.

Beautiful…
I feel manipulated by that word.
Everywhere I discern beauty,
But alone, no outer shell meets that standard.
I am reluctant to believe others
Know enough of me
To apply that label.

I know I am beautiful …
That scarred as it is,
my heart is good and compassionate;
That as analytical as it is,
my mind is expansive and open;
That when people invited in,
See all of me,
What glows out airbrushes me
To something wonderful.

So when people observing only a shell
Compliment my beauty,
My words may be "Thank you,"

But as my body and spirit prepare to flee.
My thought is "What do you want from me?"

35

Not a Goddess

You called me a goddess
Making me question
Your motives and sanity,
While considering
Your place in my heart
Repeatedly.

I am no goddess.
They're perfect in form, style and demeanor.
I am none of those things.
I'm flesh, flaws and funky frames of reference.
I can't, won't, don't see it.
It isn't so.

But I don't have your eyes,
Only my own.
I know my light
Of compassion, kindness and love
Burns bright.
Enough to obstruct your view?

Am I a piece you're collecting?
An attempt at a
Notch on your belt?
Am I naive to believe you?
Do I,

Need to believe?

A goddess would know
Her own mind and heart (I do not).
She wouldn't be wandering
Into a field
Unaware of potential bombs or
The consequences of detonation.

Maybe you see a goddess
Where none exists.
Maybe my dictionary
Incorrectly defines the term.
A meeting of our minds
Is a future hill to storm.

Here and now
The message in your eyes…
You want more than I have,
But the force is strong in you, young Jedi.

A goddess would have answers.
She would solve problems
Or easily resist,
Making it all simple and
Clear…
Yeah, pretty sure I'm not a goddess.

Alone

I told you I missed hugs.
You asked me why.
I gave you the answer
I'd been satisfying myself with.
You didn't accept it and
Made me think,
Reflect.

You made me face myself.

Yes, I live alone
And revel in the joy of it.
Yes, I can and do care for myself,
Traveling alone, having fun alone,
Cooking and eating alone.
Yes, I spend time with people
Because I choose, when I choose.

There is room for someone special.
Yes, I refuse to tolerate
Bullshit,
Gaslighting,
A lack of good humor or
Generosity.

So, I didn't lie.

But, there is more.
I am an introvert and shy
At the heart of my being.
And while, after a lifetime of trying,
I fully love and appreciate the me
I am still becoming,
In my soul
I don't believe anyone else really does.

I know it's possible …

Those men have been a part of my life,
As friends, confidants and lovers
In a variety of combinations
Sometimes all three.
So the question is:
Why not now?
Especially if I am not choosing to be without?

Nothing goes left as fast
As my making an approach.
Why does asking a man
For his number or to join me for coffee
Lead to his imagining
Me in his bed?
It's an intercourse invite, but
Verbal not sexual.

So I wait.
Wait to be noticed.
Wait to be asked.
Wait to be selected.
I am open and approachable,
More than I have been in years.
Yet no one does,
Except the unavailable.

The married… I say nope.
The betrothed… Nope.
The committed… Nope.
The unavailable… Why?

Alone it is.

Detour

It's out of the way.
The long way around.
Inconvenient.
Time consuming and a
pain in the a**.

Only if you think so.

Detours
provide times of heightened attention,
teachable moments, learning,
failure, success, and
epiphanies.

Detours are also
times of rest,
exploration,
adventure, and
peacefulness.

I am learning
to love the
detours
For the insight they bring and
the happiness I have found.

Shifting Focus

I like my skin.
It's scars and blemishes,
Unfortunate hairs on my chin…
It covers all
Though I'm not thin.
Whether too much sun or sugar
It's accepting of my sin.
Responding to good treatment to stay
Supple and soft—a big win.
I'm pretty sure it's good genes—
A nod of thanks to my kin.
Imagining you touching me
Head and heart take a spin.
The visions I conjure
Ear-to-ear grin.
My heart racing sounds like
A wooden spoon tapping tin.
If it were real
There'd be such a din.
Your skin against mine in all the right places…
My only thought now is when?

Bonded Pair

We're not a couple.
Can't be, won't be,
But we are together. That's fair.

Like peas in too small a pod,
Between synergy and bickering,
It's obvious we care.

We flirt with each other.
Occasionally, on purpose, and
Sometimes, as a dare.

We also talk ideas, history, and life.
You brighten my day when
When there's an opportunity to share.

There is nothing more, just wonderful delight.
The only way to describe us
Is as a bonded pair.

Memphis

Memphis.
I love the locale,
To visit.
It's an interesting place.

I have fun there.
Lots.
I never leave
Without a smile
And lifelong memories.

But live there?
Or keep a second residence?
No.
It's not home
For me.

Home
Is sometimes still and quiet,
Maybe even challenging.
But home lets
Me be me.

Memphis is edgy.
Feels a little dangerous.
A fun, exciting walk

On the wild side, to be
Taken in limited but regular doses.

Memphis
Makes me step up.
Requires I be bold and nimble.
Even when it's quiet and reflective,
You've gotta be ready to pivot.

I love Memphis,
But not like it hopes.
It'll never be home,
But you can always look for me there.

Selfish

I want to keep you close.
I don't know why.
You bring me joy, just not in the way you wish.
It is a joy I need and want,
But I think it brings you pain because
It isn't what you want it to be.

You have a gentle, good humor
That can be sharp when required
And you always know when.
It never fails to make me smile
And never leaves me cornered.
It is a joy I want and need.

You have a smile and look in your eye
Just for me,
And I know your pain because
They both dim a little
When reality of what we are hits you.
It isn't what you want it to be.

I love that I can count on
Seeing you.
I rarely know when
And never know why,
But it is something I have come to count on.

It is a joy I want and need.

You want to give me things
In addition to smiles, laughter,
And friendship.
I won't let you.
We can't tangle anything more.
It won't be what you want it to be.

Please stick around.
It won't ever be what I think you hope,
But it isn't and will never be nothing.
You arc a joy I need and want,
And I'm selfish enough to ask you for it.

I Don't Want to be That Woman ...

I don't want a heart
That doesn't belong to me.
Or to give my heart in a space
That is shared with another vying for the same
spot.

I don't want to be that woman.

I don't want to interject or disrupt
In order to have for myself
Something that was rightfully someone else's
Just because I am here.

I don't want to be that woman.

It doesn't matter if she knows.
What matters is she exists.
Feelings don't matter,
What matters is she exists.

I don't want to be that woman.

The woman I want to be, that I am,
Can still care about you,

Can be a friend, advisor, and support,
And stop there.

I'll be that woman.

What is Happening?

Careless
I was intrigued and giddy
When I should have been
Intentional.

Before I realized
This could be important
I was cavalier and impetuous
I didn't think.

I never took it lightly
But now I see it clearly
And worry…
"What is happening?"

Can it really be what it feels like
In this place and time?
It shouldn't be dismissed.
But should it be nurtured?

It is glistening and precious,
Rare and worthwhile.
But could birth hurt and pain
Unless I am intentional.

Mourning No More

You made me realize
I don't mourn him anymore.

I miss how his eyes
Made me feel seen.
His questions
Made me feel heard.
And how there were always
Smiles and laughter.

I didn't realize
I'd stopped living cloaked
In my grief and memories.
That I'd begun to want again
The joy of companionship.
That I was open, ready, hopeful.

Then… you made me realize
I don't mourn him anymore.

It's the Eyes

Your eyes
Sparkle
When I look at them.
I can't for too long…
I'm afraid you'll see
Something I am not sure of,
That I am not ready to handle.

You study me with those eyes.
I feel them take in
Every inch of my face,
Interpreting my reactions,
Searching for answers.

I wonder what you think
When you watch.
What it means to you…
Curiosity?
Intrigue?
Interest?

I don't think I will ever know
Because I can't look at that sparkling too long,
And I'm too hesitant to ask.

Emergence

Calm. SAFE.
I know because
My mind is still.
Void of thoughts and words.
Filled instead with the sensory.

The rapid rat-a-tat-tat of my heart
Sounds a dull thudding in my head.
But coming through my ears
It's a singing snare
In the hands of a master.

The awareness of
The gentle scrape from your palms
As they slide slowly
Down each bare arm
Makes my skin tingle everywhere.

The prick of your beard
Against my cheek and neck...
The catch in my next breath
As I bask in the pleasure
of the moment.

The husky breathless sound
As you say my name

Stills my breathing
As I wait to
Hear you say it again.

I was unsafe before.
I hid,
To prevent being so again.
The question:
Should I emerge for this?

You feel like home

You feel like home.
At all times, in all ways
You feel like home.

You feel like a summer thunderstorm,
With all the windows and doors thrown open,
Wind blowing curtains and blinds about unlit
rooms.
The drops of rain you feel standing too close to
an opening,
And the cacophony of sounds:
Raindrops pounding the sidewalk like drums;
Wind whistling through the rooms like flutes:
A melody carried by piano keys and voices.
Oh, and the peace in my core
knowing I was safe amidst it all.

You feel like home.
At all times, in all ways
You feel like home.

You feel like the lazy Sunday afternoons,
Where nothing of purpose will possibly be done
Except be around those most important to you.
With popcorn and snuggles, watching football
(or reading a book);

Or a long bike ride in the country
with mom leading and dad taking up the rear;
Or learning to play pinochle
at the dining room table,
Including the trash talking and slamming of
cards.

You feel like home.
At all times, in all ways
You feel like home.

You feel like the space I curated for myself,
Full of the things that feed my spirit,
Fuel my intellectual and creative growth,
Makes me feel strong, capable and safe.
A space of quiet courage, serenity and delight.

You feel like home.
At all times, in all ways
You feel like home.

You feel like the spaces
where I was protected and cherished,
Many and varied throughout a lifetime:
Singing with companions
as we roll down the highway;
Listening, eyes closed and body at rest,
being read to;
Making breakfast together, eating too much

and then getting in that "too full" nap;
Being listened to as I sobbed out pain
that seemed to have no end;
Being reminded that I can do and be anything
because so far there is nothing
I wanted that I haven't done or been.

You feel like home.
At all times, in all ways
You feel like home.

Home is where I want to be
In all the ways
And times
And places it presents itself.
Home, right now,
Seems to be where you are.
It is joyous and peaceful
Being there.

You feel like home.
At all times, in all ways
You feel like home.

The Third Rail

People say
Never touch the third rail.
It's where the power is,
Where the energy is surging.
Where the potency is strong enough
To knock you off your feet
And take your breath away.

The other day you walked past me
Just inside my personal space.
I felt you, like you brushed against me.

You didn't, but your aura did.
It warmed my body and
Forced a deep inhale
That caught your essence.
I needed all my strength to prevent
Swaying into you.
I felt you feel it.
You hesitated,
Stopping ever so briefly
Before continuing by.
Our eyes met and
I saw the flash
Of acknowledgement.

If that is the impact of proximity
What happens if you touch me?

Do I combust
From our mingling spirits?
Do I faint from your energy
Surging through me?
I am apprehensive about being certain;
Curious to know for sure.

This is why there is a rule
About the third rail.
It is not up for exploration.
It is not open for debate.
It is dangerous, period.
Everyone should stay away.

So, what to do?
Smart move: Avoid the situation.
Keep our spirits apart.
Let the synergy untangle and dissipate.
Be safe, survive
the journey intact.

But this is life
And the prudent move
May leave me with nothing.
Having felt the power of
Our enmeshed spirits

And the residual glow,
Do I dare not risk it,
If only for the memories?

Blur

From the slightly muffled
Boom-boom Boom-boom
Of the opening
I think of your
Heart beating strong and proud.

It makes me stop and listen
The clear melody
Ringing from the sax
Speaking for you
Drawing me into your
Space and thoughts.

Then there are
Two strong heartbeats
Almost synced
Then a blurring of
Energy, thoughts, feelings…
No need for words
An almost overwhelming connection
Inside that moment we are blurred.
Can I live inside that moment?

The sax repeats the melody but
It's me speaking
Full of joy and insecurity.

I question,
Regret my ingratitude
Then revel and let go
Being engulfed by it all.

Then there are
Two strong heartbeats
Almost synced
Then a blurring of
Energy, thoughts, feelings …
No need for words
An almost overwhelming connection
Inside that moment we are blurred.
I don't want to leave that moment.

Now that sax sings a new melody
Of our union this time.
No longer a mingling
Of energy and thought.
The notes carry to the physical. . .
My face caressing your palm
Me warm and secure
Held against your chest.
Promises being kept. . .
Plans being made. . .

Then there are
Two strong heartbeats
Almost synced

Then a blurring of
Energy, thoughts, feelings…
No need for words
An almost overwhelming connection
Inside that moment we are blurred.

Thanks Boney James.

On A Dime

I was aware I didn't know you.
How could I?
Circumstances didn't allow it.
But I was blindsided by this.

I'm a human with a past.
I can't throw the first
Or any stone.
I didn't know about or aid in wrongdoing,
But I did know the men behind some.
Questionable actions
Were not all they were,
Just as this,
I know,
Is not all you are.

I'm not sure why this hit me so hard.

It could be because I have questions
I can never have answered.
Or because I want an understanding of reasons,
Which is not my place;
I'm not your judge.
It could be because
What this means for you
Is scarier and more uncertain.

Could it be because
Holding the present moment
Isn't all that is needed?
I think it's because
The things I want for you
It's clear may never come to pass.

What If He Puts a Ring On It?

It's bare now
That second digit
From the left
On my left hand.

It doesn't need
To send sparkles
Along the ceiling
As it moves about.

Or attract attention
That signals a
Significant change
Of life status.

Is that change
Being considered?
Desired?
Sought?

What if it happened?
If he offers
Appropriate adornment,
Will it be accepted? Worn?

The second digit

Speaks volumes to the world
Without being capable of sound.
What if he puts a ring on it?

Librarian's Creed

For you
I meet each day with a smile
And a prayer for guidance
On how to be present and of service.

For you
I bring my best self:
Joy, good humor, active listening and respect,
Unafraid of the ties that bind us.

For you
I remember my lessons of growth
And share, so you may
Get what you need and learn them too.

For you
I let the Creator guide
My words and acts, then stand aside
Knowing the plan will unfold as it should.

I am
Humbled by your appreciation,
Honored by your respect and
Cherish your faith, patience and understanding.

Being here to serve
Was the Creator's gift to me.
Your acceptance of my ministrations,
Flaws and all, is my blessing from you.
Thank you.

Grateful

It's amazing.
Everything is happening
Now.

The job I've been searching for.
Opportunity to be a change agent.
Resources for all I need and some I want.
So much light inside
My outside is covered in it.
Feeling ready to accept love;
Finding interest in every direction I turn.

So much happiness and joy
In my every day
Nothing negative sticks.
So much happiness and joy
In my every day
I can create the crucial space
Needed for right action.

To ask "why now"
Seems ungrateful,
Like punching the
Proverbial gift horse in the mouth.
I'll choose to be thankful and
Feel blessed the Creator has bestowed
Love on me in this way.

"Hope Springs Eternal"

"The sun'll come out
Tomorrow."
"A journey of a 1,000 miles
begins with a single step."
"As long as you draw breath,
There is space
For things to change."

Unwavering hope.

The space where I live
Is a land of limitless opportunity
Where everything is possible,
Every dream comes true
and
"The arc of the moral universe is long,
but it bends towards justice."

I never believed
I had much patience
But truly:
"Hope,
waiting in motion,
is patience epitomized."

Unyielding hope.

"Everything will be okay in the end.
If it's not okay,
It's not the end."

My hope is limitless.

Acknowledgement and thanks to: Alexander Pope, Andrea McArdle, Lao Tzu, Martin Luther King Jr., John Lennon and me, for the quotes.